MAD ABOUT THE HOUSE

First published in the United Kingdom in 2021 by Pavilion
43 Great Ormond Street
London
WC1N 3HZ

Copyright © Pavilion Books Company Ltd 2021
Text copyright © Kate Watson-Smyth 2021

Illustration and design by Abi Read

ISBN 9781911663522

A CIP catalogue record for this book is available from the British Library.

10 9 8 7 6 5 4 3 2 1

Reproduction by Rival
Printed and bound by Toppan Leefung Pte. Ltd.

www.pavilionbooks.com

The author and the publisher have made every effort to ensure that the advice in this book is accurate and safe, and therefore cannot accept liability for any resulting injury, damage or loss to persons or property, however it may arise. It is the responsibility of the reader to ensure that all building, safety and legal regulations are met. Measurements are approximations and due diligence should always be exercised before works are undertaken.

MAD
ABOUT
THE
HOUSE

Planner
Your Home, Your Story

KATE WATSON-SMYTH

PAVILION

FOR AD, ISAAC AND NOAH – LOVE
ALWAYS. ENID, STOP SCRATCHING
THE FURNITURE.

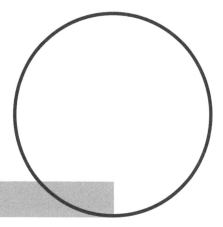

CONTENTS

YOUR HOME,
YOUR STORY

Every time I have moved house (and that's a lot of times), I have started a new notebook to keep a record of what I plan to do. Then I inevitably can't find the page where I wrote down the name of that really good paint, or the number of that really good plumber...

I also have to have another notebook of graph paper. I use this to make scale drawings of the shapes of the rooms I am designing to work out countless things, from what size sofa will fit where, to how big the kitchen table can be. And then I have to tuck that into the first notebook and it invariably falls out, taking with it the painstaking list of measurements, clever lighting schemes and priceless contacts that I have so carefully compiled.

If you're anything like me, you'll eventually end up with lots of bits of paper, several notebooks and no clue about where to find anything. And it's all very well in theory to rely on Instagram and Pinterest to be your glamorous assistants, but sometimes you just really, really need to make a note. Or a list. House renovations are all about lists.

This is the solution. *The Mad About the House Planner* has a helpful mix of graph paper for floor plans, sums and budgets, ruled paper for notes and bright ideas, and plain paper for drawings and sketches. It has checklists and space for wish lists. There are even two ribbons to help you bookmark the most useful pages for the stage you're working on. Plus, an invaluable section for you to add the contact information for your favourite trades and keep track of all the fine details, like which flooring you used where and how much it cost.

You can write the names of the Instagram accounts that provide regular inspiration, details of your favourite Pinners, and that all-important list of handy measurements: the alcove in the living room, the space between the bed and the window, the dimensions of the rug you want to buy. Never leave home without it tucked into your bag – you never know when the perfect vintage trolley might present itself. I once had to wheel one back from a routine visit to the dentist when I saw it in the junk shop next door to the surgery.

In addition to all that useful stuff, I also wanted you to be able to keep a diary of your renovation. To remember how it felt the day the wall came down (or went up), the moment the plastering was finished and the lights turned on. So, it made sense to give you a book in which you can do all that in one place – with helpful tips and advice along the way. A place where you can keep your own notes, recommendations and reminders, but also draw your own plans and record your own memories. With that in mind, the illustrations are simple outlines because your house is a blank canvas waiting for you to colour it in. Use this book to chart your journey, whether it's a rented flat or first-time purchase. Use one per house if you are a serial renovator or, if you're in your forever home, it's just a handy place to keep everything, well... handy.

I'm so excited to bring you this planner for your own renovation, redesign or even revamp, whether you are doing the corner of one room or a whole house from the ground up. Designer and architect Le Corbusier said that 'A house is a machine for living in.' And if recent years have taught us anything, it is the power that a home can wield, and the positive impact it can have on our wellbeing and productivity when we get it right. If the first book was about helping you find your style and the second answered all your design questions, this then is the book that brings everything together. The one where you write down all the ways in which your home will tell your story.

Measure any alcoves at the bottom from skirting board to skirting board. I am still furious that the chest of drawers in my office won't fit into the alcove because I measured from wall to wall: the skirting narrowed the space by a full 2cm (¾in) that just won't bend to accommodate this piece of furniture.

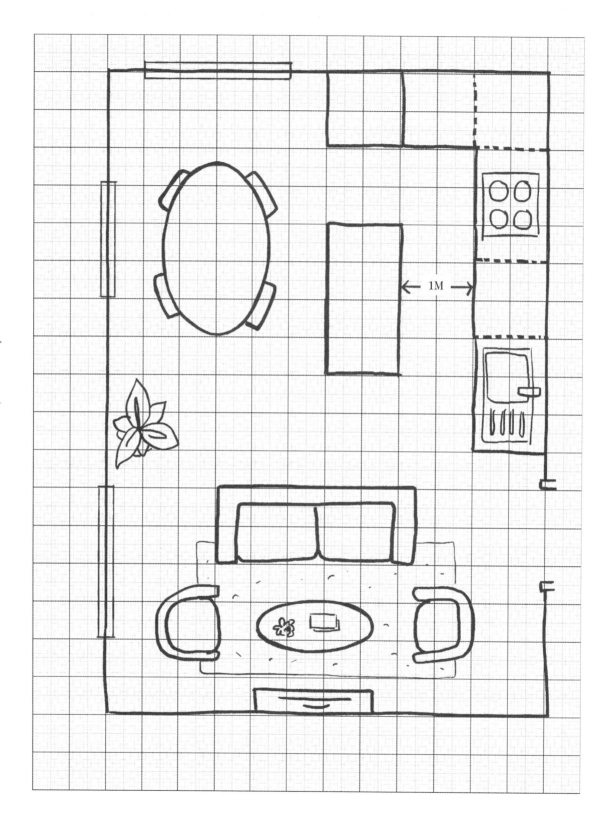

1M

ON MAKING
(FLOOR) PLANS

When I look at the particulars of houses for sale, I usually go to the floor plan before I even look at the pictures (having established that location and number of bedrooms is broadly correct). This is because you can change the décor, but you need to get a sense of the room sizes and where rooms are in relation to each other right from the start. Learning to read, and adapt, a floor plan is key, which is why this book includes pages of graph paper to help you plan your space. Here is some advice to get you started:

- On a standard floor plan, thinner lines are probably stud walls and are easier to take out. Thick lines tend to be supporting walls, which means they are basically holding the house up. You can remove them, but you'll need to add an RSJ or supporting beam and this will need to rest on something. This is why, in a classic knock-through, the opening might not go all the way across. Moving or widening internal doors also involves adding a lintel, while removing fireplaces will involve some serious propping up. So these are automatically expensive jobs.

- You always need to balance the cost of the job against any space gain. In a bedroom, for example, instead of removing the fireplace, you can perhaps box it in, create some shelving storage at the side and put the bed in front. The next owner may also thank you for not having ripped out an original feature.

- If you are planning on renovating, then a graph paper floor plan is vital. Decide on your scale – one square to 50cm (20in) for example – and draw out the room including windows and doors.

- Then you can start to plot your furniture placement. The best way to do this is to make scale cut-outs of your dining table, your sofa and your kitchen cupboards, and place them on the plan in the different combinations to see what works. Or you can draw them on and make several versions for comparison. This allows you to see at a glance if the sofa will fit between the door and the wall, or if the fridge will fit into the gap once you have added the optimum number of cupboards.

- If you are trying to work out the best size for an island or kitchen table, then you need roughly 1m (3ft) all around to allow for chairs and bar stools to be pulled in and out or for people to walk past. You can cut this distance to 80cm (31½in), about the width of a door, if it's only ever one person in the space at a time.

- Would an extra bathroom make the morning rush a little easier? Have you got room for an en suite? Use a floor plan to plot a wet room – you need about 1m (3ft) width by 2m (6½ft) length with a sliding door to save space (see page 87).

1 FIRST THINGS FIRST

This is your planning chapter. Do you want to buy only sustainable or vintage pieces? Do you want to be braver in your choices of pattern and colour, or are you putting into practice what you learnt last time? What is your red thread – the colours, materials and styles that run throughout your house linking the spaces and creating that cohesive feel otherwise known as 'home'. There are a lot of questions to answer. And here are the pages for you to do just that and to write about what you want for the place you are now inhabiting.

If you are renting with a view to buying, then now is a good time to work out what your style is. And if you are only ever going to be renting, think about what you really need from the space against any landlord-imposed limitations and work out how you can get round them. First-time buyers might be all about the balance between what you want and what you can afford. Downsizers and parents will be looking for good storage solutions, while flat-sharers will be after multi-tasking and flexible spaces.

In my last book I wrote about the six questions you need to ask yourself before you start any decoration. In short, before you start you should ask yourself: who, what, when, where, why and how? Who is doing what, where and when? Then why do you want to redo this room? And finally, how are you going to pay for it? Those questions are valid here too, and you will find a page to fill out the answers at the beginning of each chapter. The answers will vary from room to room, as different people use different spaces and have different requirements. The question pages are your starting point, where you should write down what you want, and need, overall from your home before you get into the specifics of each room. After all, the list of characters in your home may change too, and, as they grow, so their needs will change.

You must ask yourself *who* is going to be using any given room. It's not just about the members of your family. Not everyone will use every room: my teenagers have never knowingly been near the utility room, for example. It's about the type of person using any given room. So, is this a room for a toddler or a teenager, a parent or a party person, a chef or an eater, a bather or someone who prefers showers? Next you need to make a list of *what* they will be doing in the room. Are they watching TV or making conversation, working or lounging, cooking or eating? Once you know *who* is doing *what*, you can start to make the right decisions on the décor. Then you can move on to *when* they will be doing it, which will inform your lighting choices and paint colours. The question of *where* is not just about which room you are working on, but where you would like to shop. Making a list of your ideal artisan makers versus those fast-delivering corporates will inform *how* you will need to plan your budget to pay for it all.

And of course, there's the *why* – why are you doing it? Working out why a space does or doesn't work will lead you towards the things you need to fix, which will in turn help you work out the final design and make the right decisions. And that leads you to the house renovator's version of 'Kiss, Marry, Kill', or as I have renamed it, 'Lust, Love, Loathe'.

It's crucial that you make a list of what you love before you begin. If you are buying a property, make a note of what attracted you to it in the first place. This is key, not just for journaling purposes, but for that point about halfway through the process when you hate the house, hate the builders and can't imagine what possessed you to embark on such a stupid project in the first place. So, write down how the sun floods through the window at 3pm on a winter's afternoon and make a note to put a chair there. Write down how that quirky alcove brings personality to the landing and resolve not to fill it in with a characterless cupboard. Next, make a list of the things you loathe that need to come out – that hideous fireplace, those ugly fire doors and that pointless shelf in the bathroom. Write it down and tick off each item when it's gone. That will also give you a sense of achievement on a long-term project when the end seems out of sight.

But a list of loves and loathes isn't useful unless you marry them into a final list of lust, otherwise known as your goals for the space. So, if you fell in love with the large south-facing windows but loathe the dark stained carpet and would like an airy space with gorgeous billowing curtains and a parquet floor, write it all down. If you don't it will be forgotten. And it will also help you plan your budget, as you will have to decide if you want to sit on cushions on the aforementioned parquet floor for two years, or shampoo the carpet and buy that amazing sofa. So, this planner is also about working out your hopes and dreams for your home.

Finally, you must write down how you want to feel in each room because that is key to getting the décor right. If the room doesn't lend itself to billowing curtains and you can't afford a parquet floor, then you need to look for the colours and textiles that will give you that same feeling of calm and relaxation. You might love a zesty, zingy orange, but if it makes you feel energized then perhaps it's not the right shade for the bedroom walls. Why not put that shade on the stairs so it's the first thing you see when you come in? Or perhaps save it for a cushion in the bedroom, where you have learnt that a soft blue is more conducive for relaxing. For each chapter add a list of moods – you can have more than one per room – and then examine how your favourite colours make you feel to give yourself a jumping off point for your colour scheme. After all, there's no such thing as the wrong colour, just the wrong shade. This list will help you to choose wisely and ensure that you get the colour scheme right first time.

I truly believe that not enough connection is made between look and feel when it comes to decorating our rooms. My podcasting co-host Sophie Robinson adores strong, bright colours and runs successful online courses dedicated to helping you find your true colour personality. She decorated her office white to provide a calming environment that wouldn't distract from her work. Within six months she felt drained, miserable and, crucially, uninspired every time she went in there. So, she stuck bubblegum pink chintz wallpaper from House of Hackney on all four walls and painted the woodwork cobalt blue. It's a riot of colour that makes me feel slightly faint. She has never been more productive. This is proof that we all, even the experts, need to listen to our gut when it comes to decorating.

Before you move (especially if you're renting and the property might be empty), check the boiler model and download a manual because there's a strong chance the pilot light will have gone out and you need to be able to get it going for hot water and heating on the day you move in. I speak from experience: a very accommodating heating engineer (a friend of the builder) arrived and drank red wine with us while watching TV as we waited for the gas provider to ring us back with instructions.

MOVING HOUSE: A CHECKLIST

After buying, doing up and selling three houses, we were ready for a proper fixer-upper when we found our current home. The Victorian terrace had been divided into two flats and lain empty for over a year before we moved in and started the process of returning it to a single dwelling. We needed to be particularly organized on moving day for this one, so here are my (painstakingly gathered) tips.

- ☐ Now is the time to have that long-promised declutter. Make piles of things that are for the tip, recycling centre and the charity shop so you don't move them to the new house.

- ☐ Contact your utility suppliers: water, electricity, gas, landline and internet, as well as cable and satellite TV.

- ☐ Contact the post office and organize for your mail to be redirected to your new address.

- ☐ Inform the doctor, dentist, optician, gym, bank, employers and schools of your new address.

- ☐ Update your driving licence and organize parking permits if required.

- ☐ Update magazine and newspaper subscriptions.

- ☐ Make sure your insurance details are up to date.

- ☐ Buy a Sharpie (to label the boxes), bubble wrap and a packaging tape gun.

- ☐ Put together a moving day survival kit (see page 17).

- ☐ Ask the vendors for the location of useful things like water valves and stopcocks, thermostats and fuse boxes, gas and electricity meters – don't wait until there is water flooding all over the floor.

- ☐ Take meter readings at your old place and the new one.

ᴏɴ MOVING DAY SURVIVAL KITS

A good survival kit will make moving day less hellish. Packing an overnight bag (or case for the whole family) will make things less frantic on arrival – you always get the keys later than you think. Pack towels and clean clothes for all (and don't forget the toddler's teddy and pyjamas), and then you won't have to do anything other than order a takeaway and open a bottle of champagne on the night. Here is a list of items to include in your survival box:

- Must-haves include: the kettle and teabags (or cafetière), milk, phone charger and battery pack, toiletries and loo roll.
- Keep the corkscrew handy – you can buy a bottle of wine, but you need to be able to open it. Likewise, the number of the local pizza delivery (so learn your new postcode).
- It's also useful to have a couple of mugs and glasses ready for that cup of tea or glass of wine.
- Have bubble wrap, Sharpies and parcel tape at the ready – there's always something that needs packing at the last minute.
- The TV remote needs to be accessible. We moved house with a two-year-old and realized on arrival that the remote had been casually left on the bookshelves before the packers arrived. To keep him occupied while we tried to do everything else, we were faced with the task of unpacking dozens of boxes (full of around 1,000 books) to find it.
- Pack a torch. When we moved into our current house, which had been unoccupied for several months, the sockets worked but none of the overhead lights did. We hadn't checked as we had always visited in daylight. It was 10 December (almost the shortest day in the UK) and the removal men were unloading and building beds in the dark until they got to the boxes with the lamps in.
- While you don't need bedding in the survival box, try to ensure it's loaded onto the van near the end and stick a really big label on it so you can access and locate it easily. And include a few extra blankets if it's winter – our heating didn't work on that first December night.
- Keep the toolbox handy as well – you never know if you might need a screwdriver or new fuse.
- You are unlikely to have internet, so if you have children, make sure the kids have enough games or offline activities to keep them occupied.
- On a similar note, it's a good idea to get each child to pack their own survival box. Check they have included a favourite teddy, books (both reading and activity) as well as any other games. Imagine they are going on a long-haul flight and ask them what they would want.

THE SIX QUESTIONS

WHO?

WHAT?

WHEN?

You must ask and, crucially, answer these six questions honestly before you start any decorating if a room is to reflect the style and suit the needs of those who use it.

WHERE?

WHY?

HOW?

LUST, LOVE, LOATHE...

LUST

_____
_____
_____
_____
_____
_____

LOVE

_____
_____
_____
_____
_____
_____

LOATHE

_____
_____
_____
_____
_____

The interior design version of 'Kiss, Marry, Kill'. Make a note of your aspirations for the space, the great features of the room and the things you want to replace.

'Something new, Something old, Something black, Something gold.'
This mantra came about after I realized that this is, in fact, something I tend to do in every room – and I think it works.

2 THE ENTRANCE HALL

We start here because this is where you start when you come in. It's the first thing you see and we all know about the importance of first impressions. Conversely, this is the *last* place you should actually decorate because everything comes in and out this way. Many is the beautifully, and expensively, painted hall I have seen that has been battered and scuffed by incoming furniture and outgoing builders. Not to mention the trashing of the stair carpet.

This is the space that announces the people who live there. But both residents and visitors will only be passing through, so dare to go dramatic. Halls are often dark windowless spaces, so you can embrace that and go big on colour. If there are lots of doors then it's a good idea to paint the doors and all the woodwork the same colour as the walls, which will make the area look calmer and more spacious. It's also less distracting to the eye than outlining all the exits in white. Similarly, if you have coloured walls and coloured carpet then don't paint the woodwork white. Match it to either the walls or the carpet for a more seamless look. This will also make the room look bigger, as you won't be outlining the edges.

If you prefer a light and airy space (as far as is possible in a windowless corridor), think about wallpapering the ceiling or using a strong colour up there and leaving the walls pale. If your hall is narrow, bring the colour down over the top 30cm (12in) of the walls to create the illusion that the space is wider. Mirrors hung opposite doors will grab the light and throw it back out. A small narrow corridor also won't have room for furniture, so pick a gorgeous radiator and consider putting a shelf over it for flowers and mail.

If you don't have a hall but walk straight into a room, then you need to create a spot for putting down your keys and hanging up your coat so you don't end up chucking it on the sofa for the evening. In fact, whatever the size and shape of your space, storage really is key. There will be bikes. And coats. And shoes. And bags. Make a plan and then make a house rule about returning things to their rightful place. Enforce it.

For a more practical yet contemporary finish, try painting the lower half of the wall in gloss and the top in the same colour in matt. If you don't have a dado rail, another trick is to tile the bottom half of the wall and put a narrow finishing tile along the top. This will allow you to bring in the pattern of a wallpaper in a tougher, scuff-proof material that can be wiped clean.

Before you begin, remember to make a note of how you feel when you step through the front door. Now make a note of how you actually *want* to feel when you step through the front door. In other words: welcome, calm and relaxed. As if you could take off the working day like your coat and just hang it up. And then you need to think about the colours and accessories that make you feel that way.

☐ What is the first thing you see? If it's a staircase then paint or carpet it in a colour that makes you happy when you see it – and that probably isn't an oatmeal twist. Pattern hides dirt, but if it makes you nervous, paint the bannisters instead as a way of introducing some colour.

☐ If you have a view through to another room, think about that view and hang a gorgeous painting there. Or paint that wall or room a joyous colour.

☐ Storage is crucial. There probably isn't room for everyone to have all their coats and shoes in the hall. Give everyone two hooks – one for coats and one with a basket for shoes. Put a shelf over the top for a box of hats and gloves.

☐ Painting an entrance hall white won't make it lighter, but a pale colour will help it to feel airy – remember to paint all the woodwork and doors the same colour as the walls to create a calm sense of space.

☐ Consider making the ceiling the fifth wall – paint it a bold colour or hang dramatic wallpaper that will draw attention away from the narrow space.

☐ Add texture with tough textured or embossed wallpaper on the lower half of the wall, or gloss paint. You can use a contrasting or matching colour as the different finishes will add interest.

☐ If the ceiling is too low for a pendant light, hang wall lights. Or look at decorative bathroom lighting, which is often flatter and more interesting than downlights.

☐ Mirrors are vital – not just for the last-minute 'spinach in teeth' check, but to bounce any available light around.

ON HOW TO BUY
THE RIGHT CARPET

Once you've made the decision to carpet your hall, or any room come to that, the choices don't end there. Let's assume you have an idea of the colour you would like, the big question remains: what *sort* of carpet do you need? After all, the requirements for a hard-working hallway are very different from the luxurious, soft feel you might want under your bare feet in the bedroom. Work out what you need before you go anywhere near the shop and the smooth sales talk. So, it's back to those six questions. Who is using that space the most? Child or teenager? Or professionals who leave after getting dressed in the morning and don't return until bedtime. What are they doing in there? Will they be in shoes or slippers? When will they be in there? Are they passing through or staying put? Where are you carpeting? That one's easy. But why are you looking for a carpet? Does the existing one not go with the décor? Your answers will determine the wear and tear to factor in so you can choose the right sort of carpet and work out how you need to budget for it. Here's a quick guide to types, textures and colours:

- A twist, or cut pile, is the most hardwearing of them all. A twist is made, no surprises here, by twisting the strands of yarn tightly together to make it tougher. It's more resistant to crushing than a loop, which is why it is good for stairs and places where there is no furniture.
- A Berber, or loop, carpet is perfect for high traffic or busy areas. Take care if you have pets though – if they pull a loop the whole thing can start to unravel.
- Velvet, or plush, is, as the name suggests, softer and more luxurious underfoot and is made from a cut pile. This is perfect for a bedroom or dressing room.
- Once you have worked out the type of carpet you need, you get to the fun bit – choosing the colour and design. Now, patterned carpets have had a bad rap over the years, but whether it's a discreet fleck or a full-on flower explosion, a pattern will cover dirty marks better than plain. However, a pattern might mean you need to buy more to match it across joins or on curving staircases.
- Plain is always classic, so you have to decide if you are going to play it safe with a traditional neutral or if you are going to push your design boat out and go for something more dramatic. After all, you can always change the walls to suit.
- Perhaps you can have a dramatic patterned carpet and keep the walls and window dressings plain (as a change from the more traditional patterned walls and plain carpet).

THE SIX QUESTIONS

WHO?

WHAT?

WHEN?

You must ask and, crucially, answer these six questions honestly before you start any decorating if a room is to reflect the style and suit the needs of those who use it.

WHERE?

WHY?

HOW?

LUST, LOVE, LOATHE...

LUST

LOVE

LOATHE

The interior design version of 'Kiss, Marry, Kill'. Make a note of your aspirations for the space, the great features of the room and the things you want to replace.

Floorboards or tiles are the best (and easiest to clean) option for the hall. Patterned tiles will add the all-important wow factor when you open the door. Large grey tiles will look like pavement and who wants to come home to that? If you live in a first floor flat, try patterned carpet – it will hide the dirt and still bring the wow.

3 THE KITCHEN

Ah yes, the kitchen. The heart of the home and possibly either the room that sold you the house or the focus of your frustrations, as it will be the most expensive and disruptive to get right. So many hopes and dreams rest on this room and its connotations of family and home.

However, I would say it's not the kitchen that's the heart of the home but the table you put in it. That is the place where you all come together to sit and eat, to meet and plan, to row and mend hurt feelings. People need a space to gather. The Harvard Grant Study investigated the key to human happiness and found the answer lay in the formation of strong bonds with friends and family. The sustainable architect and designer Oliver Heath bases many of his designs around this idea. In his own home, the dining table is literally in the middle of the house to provide a central meeting point for everyone to come together.

A good floor plan is essential for family life, especially when it comes to kitchens. Kitchens tend to be at the back of the house with the sink in front of the window for pretty views while washing up. But in these days of open plan living, perhaps you'd rather put the working part of the kitchen (and the dishwasher) in the darker area towards the middle of the house and have the light-filled back room as a dining space. Or do you desperately want an island? Is there room? Would a peninsula be better? Using a floor plan to understand the limitations of what you have will help you correct any faults.

The kitchen is probably not the room you will start with, but it is the room you will want to redo the most. Budget restrictions, and possible building plans, often mean it has to wait a while, but that's actually no bad thing. If you really want to get the kitchen of your dreams you have to work out what's wrong with the one you already have so you can start thinking about ways to put it right. And then it isn't a question of how you should save and where you should spend. The question you need to answer is: what are the fundamental elements of the kitchen I need for the type of person I am? So, decide whether you are a cook or an eater, if you are always in the kitchen at parties or if you prefer a purely functional space. This will help you work out if you want to invest in a state-of-the-art oven or if the cooker is just for storage. Should you find the money for a wine fridge, or will a couple of vintage stools bring the party?

Just remember to treat the kitchen like any other room in the house – don't have a complete personality transplant between living room and kitchen just because it's a working space rather than a relaxing one. There is a growing fashion for kitchens to look like rooms in which you cook rather than sterile spaces full of sleek fitted appliances, so remember this when you are thinking about colours and surfaces.

Check eBay for A-Grade appliances – often you can find them in perfect working condition but they might have a scratch on the side, or damaged packaging, meaning they can't be sold at full price. It's also worth checking stores for ex-display models.

GET THE KITCHEN RIGHT: A CHECKLIST

Start by making a list of what's wrong with your current kitchen. It's just as important to know what's wrong with the space as what your dreams for it are. Use the 'Lust, Love, Loathe' pages to help you. And make sure you answer the six questions with particular focus on whom this kitchen is for and what they will be doing there.

☐ Always buy the best appliances you can afford, but don't spend lots of money on a top-of-the-range oven if you hardly ever cook. Consider a wine fridge instead.

☐ Work out how much storage you need and don't forget to allow space for the things you haven't bought yet.

☐ Check your measurements. Ideally you need 1m (3ft) for a chair to pull out from a table, and around 110cm (just over 3½ft) between an island and a worktop – less than that and it might feel too cramped.

☐ Consider the best work surface for you: wood is the cheapest but needs maintenance; natural stone is beautiful but porous so it will stain; stainless steel is practical, and what restaurants use, but gives a very industrial look. For something between the two try Caesarstone or Silestone, which are quartz surfaces that look like natural stone but are much tougher.

☐ Don't play it safe with a neutral colour unless it's your favourite shade. Base and wall cupboards don't have to match but it looks better if the darker colour is on the bottom. Remember the wall colour is easier to change than cupboard doors.

☐ Lighting is key, especially if you are eating and cooking in here. Put downlights in the work area – preferably adjustable and on a dimmer – and pendants over the dining table. Use different circuits so you can change the mood.

☐ If there is a colour that repeats itself throughout your house, bring it into the kitchen too. If you are, at heart, a maximalist, then wallpaper your kitchen and cover it with a layer of decorator's varnish to protect it from steam and splashes.

☐ To bring in your personality, think about hanging pictures or plates, or add a table lamp to the end of a worktop. Similarly, think of tiles like soft furnishings in other rooms – your chance to bring in a splash of bold colour or a pattern.

ON HOW TO MAKE A
KITCHEN
LOOK EXPENSIVE

Many of us are used to the 'shoe purchasing equation' – working out cost per wear and coming up with a figure so justifiably cheap that it would be a crime not to buy. Kitchens can work on the same principle except we really do use them every day. This means that you need to get it right if you're going to justify the cost and love the room for a long time. But that doesn't always mean you have to spend a fortune. Focusing on the details can make a modest kitchen look more expensive and you will also be creating a space that is a perfect reflection of your style and needs. And that, surely, is priceless.

- You can begin with affordable cabinet carcasses such as Ikea or Howdens; the latter come ready-assembled, so that's a couple of days of labour you don't have to pay the builder for. Instead, pay him to make new doors you can paint, so you can change them later if you fancy. Then add your own handles – prices range enormously as there is so much choice, but it's always good to invest in the touch points.

- Always spend money on things with working parts like taps, light switches and ovens.

- Paint bottom cupboards in a different colour from wall cabinets. It will look bespoke and more expensive.

- Instead of wall cupboards, consider open shelves filled with the prettiest things you use every day – plates, mugs, glasses, storage jars and serving platters. You could make them from old scaffolding boards and buy statement brackets, or create a series of cubbyholes from MDF and paint them to match the wall so they disappear and your stuff stands out.

- Good lighting will hide a multitude of cheap decorating sins. Make sure you install a dimmer and put different areas of the room on different circuits so you can hide the washing up while you're eating.

- Splashbacks are often small so, ahem, splash out on fabulous tiles or even some antique mirror that will bounce the light around. This will elevate the whole space.

- If you have open shelving (or glass-fronted cupboards) then decant large packets of dry goods into pretty jars and label them.

- A group of (well-watered) herbs in pots or a single leafy plant (as large as you can fit) will always bring a sense of luxe to any room.

- If you are redoing a kitchen on a tight budget, do try and integrate as many of the appliances as possible – a run of cupboards will look instantly more expensive than a dishwasher and a washing machine.

THE SIX QUESTIONS

WHO?

WHAT?

WHEN?

You must ask and, crucially, answer these six questions honestly before you start any decorating if a room is to reflect the style and suit the needs of those who use it.

WHERE?

WHY?

HOW?

LUST, LOVE, LOATHE...

LUST

_____
_____
_____
_____
_____
_____

LOVE

_____
_____
_____
_____
_____
_____

LOATHE

_____
_____
_____
_____
_____
_____

The interior design version of 'Kiss, Marry, Kill'. Make a note of your aspirations for the space, the great features of the room and the things you want to replace.

Consider painting the insides of your cupboards in a bright contrasting shade that makes you feel energized when you open them.

4 THE BATHROOM

Conversely, as this is chapter 4, this is the room you *should* start with. Why? Because when the house is full of builders and you don't have a kitchen, you need this space to wash your plates and wash your body and, *in extremis*, wash the tears away. Also, there's often a lock so you can hide from demanding pets, whining toddlers and disgruntled partners. If you take nothing else from this book, remember this: decorate your bathroom first.

And the second thing you need to remember is that, just like the kitchen, you need to approach this room as if it were any other room in your house. In other words, just because the furniture is preordained and probably white, that doesn't mean you have to desert your normal taste and go with wall-to-wall aqua tiles or modern vanity units just because it's a bathroom.

You can incorporate the colours and patterns you like in tiles, towels and window dressings (should you have a window). If you have floorboards throughout the house, you can install porcelain tiles that look like floorboards in the bathroom. If you love bright patterns and colour clashes then look for tiles that reflect your style. If your style tends towards vintage, consider installing a basin on an old table from eBay, or sourcing an old cupboard for storage, or even some antique shelves or a mid-century modern stool for resting that glass of wine when you're bathing.

If you're worried about your bathroom falling out of fashion, stick to classic black and white and bring the colour with the towels. But while coloured bathroom suites may not be taking off in the way the trend forecasters would have us believe, there's nothing to stop you painting the ceiling or walls in a dramatic 'non-bathroom' colour. My bathroom is dark green with pale pink woodwork, which are colours that appear elsewhere in my house, so it feels cohesive and part of the overall scheme. Again, just because it's a bathroom doesn't mean you can't incorporate your style and personality in the same way you would do in any other room of the house.

Put wall lights either side of the mirror. They are more flattering than an overhead beam and you'll have more confidence to face the day having seen yourself in the best light – literally.

PLAN THE PERFECT BATHROOM: A CHECKLIST

The six questions are vital here – is this a busy family bathroom or a relaxing retreat? Is it for showering or bathing? Remember to think ahead when planning a bathroom, as your needs may be different in a few years.

☐ Do you really need a bath or would a walk-in shower be better? Sometimes a really big shower is more luxurious than a small bath with a shower over.

☐ Have you got room for two basins? That's one less argument in the morning.

☐ Think about how much storage you need and double it. When you run out of floor space for storage, use the walls.

☐ If you want a bath, choose one with a thin edge that will give you more space to bathe in without taking up more room. If you have a shower over a bath, it's worth investing in a cast iron or resin bath, as acrylic baths can flex and drop over time, leading to a leak between the silicon joint and the edge of the bath.

☐ A wall-mounted toilet will make the space look bigger (as you'll see more floor) and be easier to clean around. Use the space above for shelving and storage.

☐ Spend on working parts that come into contact with water – taps, shower screens and trays, and basin parts. Buying the best you can afford will save you money in the long run.

☐ You don't have to use the same tiles throughout. Consider a patterned splashback and something plain on the floor. Tiles that look like wooden floorboards work well to link en suite bathrooms to bedrooms.

☐ Underfloor heating is worth the extra expense in a bath or shower room. Not least because heated towel rails tend to only heat the towels not the room, and radiators take up precious wall space. If you are going for a wet room style then, at the very least, put heating under the shower tiles on the floor – this will dry the water faster and protect the grout from limescale and soap staining.

☐ Every bathroom looks better with a bit of vintage wood to soften the space, so think about adding a shelf, bench or a cupboard.

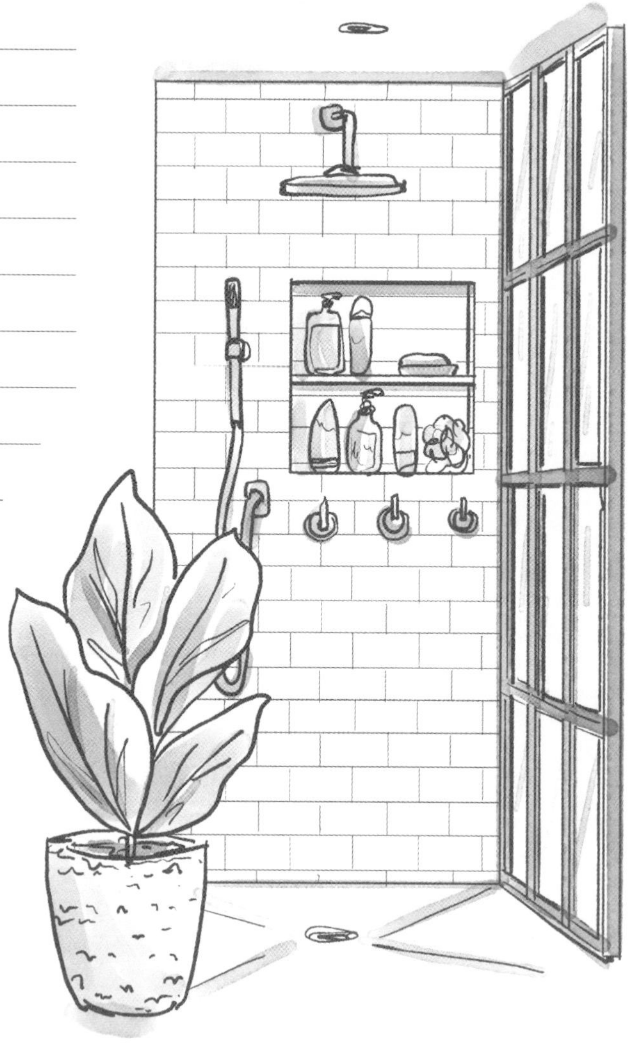

ON PLANNING
A BATHROOM

The average UK bathroom is 8ft by 6ft. When you consider that the size of a standard bath (5ft by 2ft) is only slightly smaller than a standard single mattress, you can see it's a tight fit. Given that showering was a mostly European habit until the 1990s, most of the UK has a shower over the bath, unless they pull out the latter or convert a bedroom into a larger bathroom. When you have to cram a lot of function into a tiny space, it can be easy to forget to add character. Someone recently said that bathroom décor is key because it's 'where you start and end your day'. I thought that was such a good point. From stumbling in on a wet working morning to floating in for a relaxing evening facial or soak, this room reflects all our moods back at us, so it's worth giving it a chance to influence them as well. Here are my tips on planning a bathroom with personality:

- Colour is always going to be the easiest way to add character. Don't forget that the bathroom is a room in your house and needs to look like it belongs there. So make a list of your key style notes (or your red thread) and make sure you incorporate some of those details in your colour scheme.
- Consider softening the hard edges with vintage wood and lots of plants.
- Soften the space further with the three Cs: curves, curtains and colours. Make the shapes as round and soft as you can. Perhaps add a shower curtain or window dressings.
- Lighting is crucial in a bathroom. I don't have wall lights (although I rather wish I did), but I have my downlights on a dimmer, so I can create a more relaxed atmosphere when I choose.
- If you need to have a shower over the bath then choose a bath with

vertical sides so you have more standing room (rather than a bath with sloping sides).
- If you choose to have a walk-in wet-room-style shower, then have the biggest fixed showerhead your water pressure will take and add a hand-held attachment as well, as this makes cleaning easier.
- If you are creating a wet room (where the floor slopes to the drain), you may not need a shower screen as long as any furniture is outside the splash zone – typically 70 per cent of the water lands within 60cm (23½in) of the showerhead. But while you might not mind a wet basin, you don't want a wet loo seat.
- Finally, consider a coloured suite. It's been a slow burn – I remember writing about them at least three years ago, but they are coming. And you will succumb – if not to a bath, then in the downstairs loo for sure.

THE SIX QUESTIONS

WHO?

WHAT?

WHEN?

You must ask and, crucially, answer these six questions honestly before you start any decorating if a room is to reflect the style and suit the needs of those who use it.

WHERE?

WHY?

HOW?

LUST, LOVE, LOATHE...

LUST

_____
_____
_____
_____
_____
_____

LOVE

_____
_____
_____
_____
_____
_____

LOATHE

_____
_____
_____
_____
_____
_____

The interior design version of 'Kiss, Marry, Kill'. Make a note of your aspirations for the space, the great features of the room and the things you want to replace.

Don't assume the bedroom should be big and the bathroom small. The other way around can be more luxurious and feel more 'hotel'.

5 ᵀᴴᴱ LIVING ROOM

In many ways this is the easiest room to tackle as, other than a sofa, you don't have to buy specific furniture or have anything made to fit. But it can also be the hardest as it has no set purpose and its function will change from house to house. We are all generally agreed that this is a room for relaxing, but how one achieves that precious state of mind will vary for each and every one of us.

If the kitchen table is the heart of a home, then the living room is, in microcosm, *your* home's personality. It is probably the room with the most pictures on the wall and the most family photographs, familiar objects and souvenirs. It is where you come to relax and gather around the fire (if you have one). If the kitchen is where everyone heads to do their own thing – cooking, homework, eating dinner, a little bit of admin – then the living room is where everyone comes to share an activity – a drink, a conversation, a film or favourite TV show. You have to make this room work for you and the people you live with.

This is one of the most important rooms for the six questions. And yet, because it's called 'the living room', so often people just throw in a three-piece suite and a feature wall and leave it at that. Later, perhaps when the teenagers have retreated to their bedrooms, you realize that the colour of the sofa is too sensible to spark anyone's joy and too uncomfortable to watch TV. The coffee table is too far away to retrieve a mug or rest your feet, while the wooden blinds make the room feel cold and cut out most of the available light. That's why here, more than in any other room, it's important to make a list of how you want to feel, work out the mood you want to achieve and work backwards from there. Yes, it might seem obvious: relaxed, comfortable, happy, calm and chatty. You want to feel all the emotions that basically sum up the idea of 'home'. But only once you have identified the feelings you want to experience in here can you start to work out the colours, shapes, textiles and objects that will engender those emotions.

That's where the work is in this case, and where Pinterest can be really helpful. Rather than just pinning a whole load of pictures you like, take the time to go back and ask yourself what it is you like about them. Does that paint colour make you feel calm or energized? If it's the latter, perhaps that's a better colour for the kitchen. Is that glass coffee table practical, or is the four-year-old going to smash a wooden truck through the top of it? (Yes, that was a phase…) And yes, they will grow up, and yes, they can learn, but you can always buy a new coffee table in a few years when they never come out of their bedroom and save yourself the stress in the meantime.

Two final pieces of advice here, one of them mine, the other from Michelle Ogundehin: buy the biggest rug you can afford, and the biggest sofa you can fit – it should be like a hug every time you sit down.

Buy the biggest rug you can afford or layer them up. Front legs of sofas should always be on the rug, and avoid rug islands with coffee table boats sailing on them please. If you are in rented accommodation and want to cover a dubious carpet then you need to make sure the door will still open over a rug sitting on top of it. If you want to layer smaller rugs, then a classic black-and-white striped rug (lots of places do them) will work well with a couple of plain ones, which you can match to cushions to make it look like it was a design plan and not a budget issue.

WHERE TO START WITH A LIVING ROOM: A CHECKLIST

Home isn't always necessarily a place, it's a feeling. This is the room that symbolizes home, so don't forget to list the feelings you want to experience here before you begin.

☐ When it comes to choosing a colour, remember to make a list of how you want to feel in this room and work out which colours encourage that feeling.

☐ Paint the skirting boards, doors and radiators to match the walls to make the space feel larger and calmer.

☐ Make sure your sofa is fit for *your* purpose, whether that's a family gathering or a formal spot for drinks and grown-ups. In a small room, consider choosing a sofa the same colour as the walls, which will create a sense of space, as the two will blend together.

☐ If at all possible, don't put all the furniture around the edge of the room or it will look like a doctor's surgery. Pulling a chair forward even a few inches will create the illusion of space.

☐ Plan the furniture layout before you work out the lighting scheme (see page 144 for advice). Downlights should be on a dimmer, if you'd like them, to create atmosphere. Put them about 30cm (12in) in from the edge of the ceiling where they can highlight bookshelves or art. Alternatively, place them over the middle of the windows to wash light down over the curtains or blinds.

☐ Floor sockets mean you can put a lamp at the end of the sofa, or on a table behind it, without having trailing cables.

☐ Think about where the TV should go. Putting it over the fireplace will probably mean it's too high for you to see it comfortably.

☐ When hanging pictures, try to ensure the middle of the picture is roughly at eye level. Also try to make sure the top of the picture isn't level with the top of the door – you need to vary the levels a bit to avoid creating too many straight lines.

☐ Make sure the coffee table is big enough for the room and fit for your purpose, whether that's art books, cocktails or feet.

ON BUYING
VINTAGE FURNITURE

Just as fashion is cyclical, so furniture trends will work their way back round. In the 1990s, no one wanted so-called 'brown' or antique, furniture, but with the current (welcome) moves towards design sustainability, vintage is making a comeback. Whether you splurge on mid-century or antique, or just pick up some cheap pine tables you can paint, it pays to have a few tricks up your sleeve to secure a good deal.

- There is no substitute for time spent on research. We're all familiar with the phrase 'throw money at it'. That's what happens when you don't have time to shop and/or to seek out the best prices. I'm often asked how to save money when it comes to furnishing our homes, and the truth of the matter is that time is your best friend. You need to be able to set aside a couple of hours to search online or even a few days to visit antique fairs and car boot sales. If you're in a hurry, you're just going to throw money at the nearest department store and be done with it. If it really matters to you, take the time to look for what you really want and then find the best deals.

- If you're shopping online, be very specific about your search terms. If you want six chairs, say so – or you'll have to wade through pages offering two or four. Tick as many boxes relating to period, material and type of furniture as you can. And, on eBay, head to the Advanced search menu and make sure you tick the 'used' box and enter 'original' in the keywords if you don't want to be deluged with 'vintage style'.

- Technically, antique means anything over 100 years old and vintage is anything over 20, but not everyone abides by that so don't be afraid to have a chat with the seller. Many own bricks-and-mortar shops as well as dealing online and are passionate about their work. If they don't have what you're looking for, they may be able to source it. They might also take a cheeky offer if you show genuine interest and appreciation for their stock.

- Try running a search with spelling errors. There's a website called FatFingers that shows you the most common eBay spelling mistakes. We all make them, and it would be galling to miss out on a really good price for an Eames chair because you didn't search for 'Eemes'.
- If you are looking for something specific, set up eBay and Google alerts, but be prepared to move fast when something comes up.
- Always double-check the size of the thing you are buying online. I've come unstuck with that so many times. Fortunately, this doesn't tend to matter so much when it comes to small pieces (vases and pots, for example). But if you are buying a chair, make sure you check how tall the back is – can you rest your head if you want to? How tall are the legs? Is it a small chair for sitting upright or a wide one for curling up in? All these things must be checked before you hand over your credit card details because, even if you can return it, it's a right royal pain, not to mention a waste of all that time as you will have to start again.
- Don't forget you can always reupholster and repaint. You might find a battered armchair for £10, so spend some money getting it remade in the fabric of your choice. We once grabbed a fabulous table from the side of the road that was hideously varnished and tatty. After a quick rub down with some sandpaper and disinfectant it looks great. So, don't rule out something really cheap if you think you can make something of it.
- If you're offline, get to your chosen market either really early to beat the crowds, or take a punt that there will be good stuff left at the end of the day. If you're an early bird and arrive when it's all just warming up, you may strike a good deal by offering fast and setting the seller's day off to a good start. Alternatively, if you arrive late, sellers might take a lower offer in order to clear their stock. It's tough to find a bargain these days. Sellers know the value of their stock and the demand for it. The days of picking up a genuine Wassily chair for £50 at a car boot sale or flea market are well and truly over (although I know someone who did). But you can score if you arrive at the right time.

THE SIX QUESTIONS

WHO?

WHAT?

WHEN?

You must ask and, crucially, answer these six questions honestly before you start any decorating if a room is to reflect the style and suit the needs of those who use it.

WHERE?

WHY?

HOW?

LUST, LOVE, LOATHE...

LUST

_____
_____
_____
_____
_____
_____
_____

LOVE

_____
_____
_____
_____
_____
_____

LOATHE

_____
_____
_____
_____
_____
_____

The Living Room

The interior design version of 'Kiss, Marry, Kill'. Make a note of your aspirations for the space, the great features of the room and the things you want to replace.

Layer your lights – you must have overhead, floor, table and task. A dimmer is essential.

6 THE MAIN BEDROOM

The temptation for most of us is to take the largest bedroom for ourselves and put the kids in smaller rooms. But, think about it. I'm guessing that you don't have a huge pile of plastic tat including a play kitchen or a train set. Do you also have to sleep with 47 cuddly toys that need space on the floor when they are kicked off in the night? In our last house, we put the boys in the largest bedroom in bunk beds, with cupboards in the alcoves and lots of floorspace to play. We took the second bedroom, which was perfectly big enough for our bed and clothes storage.

If you don't share your house with others then by all means take the biggest bedroom, but consider how you are using the space. It may be that you can install a false wall behind the bedhead, which you can use to create a wardrobe that will hide all the clutter. As well as providing lots of storage, it allows you to leave just the bed in your sleeping area, so it will be tidier and more zen and you will sleep better. All-round win. In period houses, the obvious solution is to build wardrobes in the alcoves either side of the fireplace, but they are rarely deep enough for this and will stick out. This also often means you have a huge amount of space around the bed that isn't doing anything and not enough room for your clothes. Take a few minutes to think about what you need from this room and make notes to help you decide.

As well as storage, also consider colour. If you love colour and pattern and feel you would like stronger colours in your bedroom, consider putting them behind your bed (or on the bedhead) so that you don't see them when you are lying down. And when it comes to textures, think about a deep-pile rug or carpet underfoot, crisp cotton or soft linen sheets and a velvet bedspread. It needs to feel plush and cosy in here. And, it's perfectly possible to do that within a neutral colour palette if that is what you prefer. It can look monastic and calm but it still needs to feel fabulous. In a small characterless room, or if you have a plain divan bed, why not use paint or wallpaper to create the feel of a luxurious canopied bed. Paint, or paper, a strip as wide as the bed up to the ceiling and across, ending roughly where the bed ends.

When choosing the colour consider if you are an owl or a lark – the former might prefer dark cosy colours, the latter will want something bright and airy to wake them up in the morning. Soft calming colours work better than bright energizing shades.

There is talk nowadays of a sleep crisis. We're all too wound up and working too hard to take the time for those essential seven hours. So what is to be done to encourage good sleeping habits? Getting the décor right can really help – by encouraging you to go to bed earlier so you can enjoy the room. Here are some tips on how to achieve a relaxing, luxurious and clutter-free space.

☐ Built-in wardrobes will give you 30 per cent more storage than freestanding. Build them up to the ceiling and match them to the wall colour so they don't make the room feel smaller.

☐ Consider the position of the pendant light – the middle of the ceiling may mean the light hangs pointlessly over the end of the bed. If so, move it. Buy a long length of coloured electrical flex and ask an electrician to rewire the light. Fix a cup hook in the ceiling where you want the light to hang, then drape the flex across from the original fitting and let it hang from there.

☐ If space is tight then using wall lights (or hanging bedside lamps as above) will do away with the need for bedside tables.

☐ If you don't have room for bedside tables, consider a shelf over the bedhead but keep it narrow so you don't bang your head and remember to make sure the tallest person can sit up.

☐ A bespoke bedhead the width of the whole wall, with tables in front, will make the room look bigger.

☐ Either buy a rug that fits under the whole bed or two smaller bedside ones. Avoid one that just goes under the foot of the bed – it's pointless and looks odd.

☐ Use blackout blinds for practicality, but add curtains for décor. A velvet Roman blind with a blackout lining is good middle ground.

☐ Buy the biggest bed you can fit into the room. You will only ever be glad of this. Likewise, buy the best mattress you can afford.

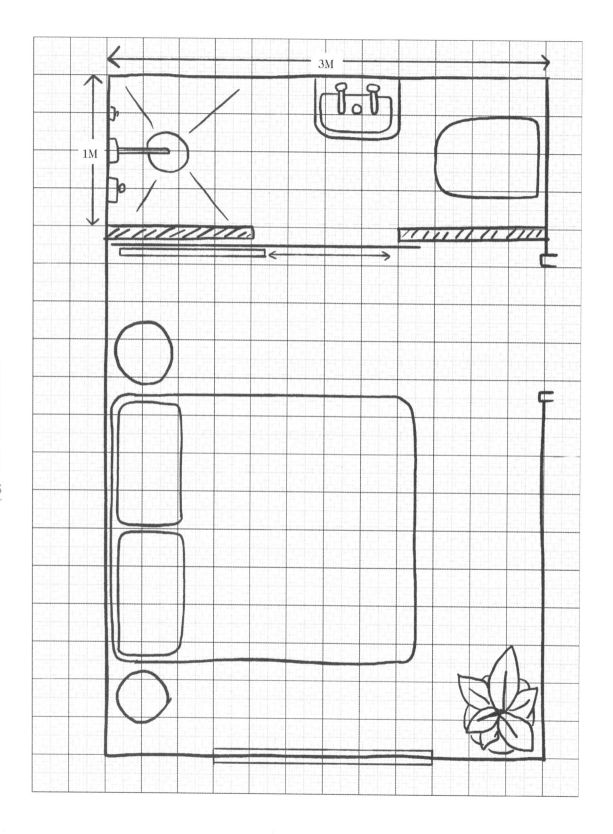

ON PLANNING THE LAYOUT

Ideally, the bedroom would only be used for its primary purpose of sleeping (and can actually be moved to the smallest room as washing and dressing has been put elsewhere). Often this isn't possible and I've seen bedrooms where enormous wardrobes loom over the bed or where a tiny en suite has been crammed into the corner, which makes the bedroom cramped and the showering experience miserable. What we are really looking for is a sense of space and luxury. If you need to include an en suite, you can create that 'hotel' feel with careful planning and a clever floor plan. Here are some space-saving and layout tips.

- Ask the builder if you can steal any space from a nearby bedroom to make the en suite slightly bigger. If it's a stud wall this won't be too expensive or difficult.
- Consider borrowing light from the rest of the room by taking the walls three quarters of the way up and using glass for the top, which won't affect privacy.
- Sliding doors are more expensive to fit but take up much less space. They are nearly always worth the investment.
- If your room is 3m (10ft) long and you can spare 1m (3ft) off the length, you can add an en suite. Create a rectangle across the end of the room with a shower at one end, the loo at the other and a basin between the two. A standard shower tray is 800 x 800mm (31½ x 31½in) and a loo ideally needs the same width. A standard pan will also project 570mm (22½in) into the room, but a compact one (which basically loses that white part behind the seat so doesn't affect the seating area) is between 450mm (17¾in) and 480mm (19in), so that represents a decent space saving in a small room. Requirements insist on 760mm (30in) around you for clearance but, again, a metre is ideal.
- You always need more storage than you think in a bathroom so if you run out of floorspace go vertical and use the walls.
- Remember, don't put downlights in a grid on the ceiling but think about where light is needed; wall lights either side of the mirror are more flattering.
- Using the example floor plan and the measurements provided here as a guide, head over to the floor plan page and use the graph paper to plot your space.
- A quick final note on colour. As this is an en suite, keep a colour connection with the bedroom. This could be with paint, or perhaps the bedspread could match the bathroom window blind, or the towels the bedroom curtains.

THE SIX QUESTIONS

WHO?

WHAT?

WHEN?

You must ask and, crucially, answer these six questions honestly before you start any decorating if a room is to reflect the style and suit the needs of those who use it.

WHERE?

WHY?

HOW?

LUST, LOVE, LOATHE...

LUST

_____
_____
_____
_____
_____
_____

LOVE

_____
_____
_____
_____
_____
_____

LOATHE

_____
_____
_____
_____
_____
_____

The interior design version of 'Kiss, Marry, Kill'. Make a note of your aspirations for the space, the great features of the room and the things you want to replace.

Before you rush out or go online to buy something new, take the time to 'shop your home' for an item that might work in the space.

7 THE SECOND BEDROOM

For some, the second bedroom will need to be a nursery, and this is where excited first-time parents spend the most money when the baby could have slept in a drawer. It's completely understandable, but be aware that decisions made about this room are mostly about you. Before your first child you swear there will be no plastic tat, only tasteful wooden toys. By the time you have your second, you realize that being hit over the head with a wooden mallet is much more painful than being attacked with a plastic one. And of course, I know that *your* child would never hit anyone, but it may be hit by someone else's.

When you are pregnant you can spend hours colour coordinating all those gorgeous clothes on tiny wooden hangers with smiling faces. When the baby actually arrives, you will very quickly realize that that's a job for magazine stylists only. Now, I don't want to take anyone's joy from this period – I did this myself – but be aware that it's a transitory moment and requirements will change.

If you are lucky, your beautifully planned nursery will last until they go to 'big school' at the age of four or five, at which point they will want a change. When friends start coming round for play dates they'll want the 'babyish' stuff gone. And it's also at this point that it becomes all about the storage, as the toys just get bigger and bigger and take up more and more space. The school books and clothes have also started arriving, so consider how you might include adaptable storage solutions (see page 99 for ideas). This new bedroom should last until they really go to big school, i.e. high school. It is at this point that you need a secret cupboard for the Lego that they probably still want to play with but don't want their mates to see, and the teddy bear that probably still sleeps in the bed but needs to hide when anyone comes round. We will deal with that stage in Chapter 8.

It's vital to get them on board from the start and to help them feel some ownership of the space. Let them choose their colours by all means but give them a pre-edited list to choose from – that way you know you won't hate the end result. Encourage them to feel 'bedroom proud' and they might look after their room and the things in it a little more. Yes, we can all dream... But in the meantime, know this: only parents use hangers.

One of the easiest and most effective storage methods is wooden Shaker pegs, which are long and can take several hangers or the handles of a chunky basket. Fit them all the way around the room. This is not only decorative but will also mean kids can hang up clothes. My son had a row of seven: five pegs for white school shirts and two for the weekend, so he could see what was going on at a glance. They also work brilliantly for school bags, shoes, pictures, bags of toys, and laundry. Later they (or, more likely, you) can put hangers on them with clothes, which helps keep the floor clear.

HOW TO PLAN A KID'S BEDROOM: A CHECKLIST

Storage is absolutely paramount in here. Kids can sleep on a mattress on the floor but they must have easy access to toys (for taking out and putting away), as well as clothes. And leave extra space for the toys they will acquire.

☐ Open boxes and baskets are much easier than drawers for small people. They can throw in toys and laundry from across the room and are more likely to do that than go to the bother of opening a drawer or removing a lid – trust me on that, I have two boys.

☐ If the room is small, use the walls for storage. Cabin beds with storage underneath are great. Built-in desks along a wall with wall lights above and drawers underneath can be a real space saver. This is a room where a friendly carpenter can really help you make the most of the space.

☐ Putting a desk in a cupboard (or built-in wardrobe) is a good way to be able to close it off at the end of the day. Just as adults don't want to look at a reproachful desk all evening, nor do kids.

☐ Create the largest notice board you can – cork, chalk or whiteboard. This will do for messages and reminders as well as pinning artwork and drawings.

☐ Use a paint with a slight sheen that you can wipe – no chalky finishes in here.

☐ You don't have to paint all four walls from skirting to ceiling in the same colour in here. Consider using paint to zone the space: a yellow triangle from the ceiling to the floor around a corner (like a beam of light) for a desk, a green area around the window for sitting and reading. This also works to zone individual spaces in a shared room.

☐ Blackout blinds are non-negotiable, but don't worry if they allow some light around the edges – that will allow a more natural waking time.

☐ Carpet is both soft and comfortable for floor play, but it won't like food and drink. Either make a rule about that or resolve to buy a cheap carpet for the early years and replace it later (not that it's any easier to get beer and pizza stains out). It also provides soundproofing for the room below.

ON LETTING
CHILDREN CHOOSE
THEIR OWN DÉCOR

Children's rooms can be tricky. My sons are now 18 and 20 and when they were born – in 2001 and 2003 – it was still basically only possible to get football or fairies for bedroom décor. There was the odd dinosaur or pirate, but it was pretty generic and I refused point-blank to allow cartoon characters in their bedroom. Yes, I was that parent. Don't @ me, as they say. That said, I strongly disapprove of grey bedrooms for kids. They need to be able to express themselves and they tend to be drawn to bright colours. So where is the compromise?

- The problem is, when you have spent so much time and effort on the rest of your house, you don't want your kids' rooms to look like they are part of a different universe. The key is to find a middle ground that they like and you can tolerate. That is the balance of power in this instance. This is their space.

- If bright colours aren't your thing, consider showing them the Farrow & Ball palette. Most of the colours have a dollop of grey to make them more muted and 'dirtier'. There are still bright oranges and pinks and yellows, but it's not that shiny pastel ice cream palette.

- If they are insisting on purple walls, suggest painting a large purple square on one wall and putting all the artwork within it, then perhaps add some matching shelves. If they want lots of bright colours, consider a bold wallpapered ceiling to keep the walls calmer.

When my children started to make decisions about their rooms for the first time – at around the age of 12 – the elder wanted lime green and black. We allowed the black carpet on the basis he would clean it (we had about a 50 per cent success rate), and one lime green wall, which I chose. I told him it was the only lime green paint in the shop! We both felt we had won. The younger one wanted blue walls and a yellow carpet to 'make a beach'. I couldn't find yellow carpet so we settled for a really cheap orange one, which was hideous. But he was constantly making and painting and is incredibly untidy, so he managed to trash it fairly quickly and I didn't care. We replaced it with a charcoal one that was much better quality a few years later. Once again, we both felt like we were winning – he had something new and I had something that didn't hurt my eyes.

THE SIX QUESTIONS

WHO?

WHAT?

WHEN?

You must ask and, crucially, answer these six questions honestly before you start any decorating if a room is to reflect the style and suit the needs of those who use it.

WHERE?

WHY?

HOW?

LUST, LOVE, LOATHE...

LUST

_____
_____
_____
_____
_____
_____

LOVE

_____
_____
_____
_____
_____
_____

LOATHE

_____
_____
_____
_____
_____
_____

The interior design version of 'Kiss, Marry, Kill'. Make a note of your aspirations for the space, the great features of the room and the things you want to replace.

_____

_____

_____

_____

_____

_____

_____

_____

_____

_____

_____

_____

_____

_____

_____

_____

_____

_____

Layered lighting is key: a strong central overhead light will give them enough to play and find that missing Lego, but don't forget to add both desk and bedside lamps. The gentle glow of fairy lights or a night light can also promote relaxation.

8

THE **THIRD BEDROOM**

This chapter is all about the third bedroom or 'spare' room. It might be a guest room that doubles as a home office or dressing room, or it might be the scene of that first teenage makeover. One tip for a space that doubles as a guest room is to make sure you buy a desk with drawers; you can put the laptop and pens in a drawer and replace them with the mirror and trinket tray you have stored there. This means you can quickly swap the look from working room to guest room. (For more tips on creating a great guest room see page 113. For more tips on creating a home office, see Chapter 9.)

The first teenage makeover often happens in here just before, or just after, they start high school, at around the age of 12 or 13. It should last until they are 18, when they may leave home for university or college, at which point you have a part-time guest room and a place to dry the laundry. So this is the point at which you need to create a space where they will not only want to relax and hang out with mates, but also study for, arguably, the most important exams of their lives. So, a proper work area with a desk is paramount. As is a good chair, which will probably double up as the chair they use for screen time. All in all it will get a lot of use, so buy a good one. They will want speakers and the ability to play music, too, so factor that in. If you can fit a double bed in, it's a good idea. If the bed needs to sit against a wall, teenagers often want a hangout space so a bed that can be filled with cushions to look more like a sofa is a good idea. Then they can all relax in a space that's more bedsit than bedroom. Or buy a sofa bed, but be aware that they won't fold it away every morning like you would if it was yours.

At this stage they might be considering hangers for shirts, tops and dresses, so factor this in. If you have the Shaker pegs from the previous chapter, those will still work and can accommodate several hangers. Otherwise a freestanding clothes rail works really well. Teenagers can regard their clothes as decoration and might like to see them. The LA-based fashion and streetwear designer Chris Stamp collaborated with Ikea on a collection of see-through and display storage. He understood that if you are spending a lot of money on trainers, you don't necessarily want to hide them in a cupboard out of sight. And, just as small kids won't use hangers, teenagers won't use drawers. They will need a second, smaller chair to drape all those clothes that are between wash and wear, because they won't be put away. Be aware of this – it will make your life less stressful and give you more space for that chair.

Many boys have a massive growth spurt and suddenly struggle to fit into a standard single bed, which is 6ft long. Mine didn't – he was more of a slow and steady type and was still going (or growing) at 18. When his childhood mattress needed replacing we bought a new single. Three months later, all his friends had double beds and I wasn't about to shell out for a whole new bed and a second mattress… So if you're looking to replace your teenager's mattress and have the space, future-proofing their sleeping arrangements is definitely something to think about.

CLEVER CHOICES FOR SPARE ROOMS: A CHECKLIST

The key thing to remember is that multi-tasking furniture is your friend here. A desk with drawers will allow you to store a mirror and trinket tray in one, and a laptop, pen and paper in the other, while a good sofa bed is an excellent space saver.

☐ If your teenager has moved out – partially at least – it might be time to invest in that aforementioned sofa bed or, for a small room, a chair bed. This will be comfortable for visits home and free up space if the room is now mainly used for working, guests, exercise bikes or laundry dryers.

☐ If you're redecorating the space as a guest room, push the boat out, as no one will be in here often. Use the wallpaper or bold paint colour you didn't dare to before.

☐ There is no need for a bulky wardrobe in a guest room. They take up huge amounts of space and are inefficient storage solutions. Instead, put some pretty hooks on the wall and leave a few hangers (wooden or more decorative, not wire) for guests to hang their clothes on.

☐ Remember, most teenagers just won't use a chests of drawers. And guests very rarely do. Most clothes can be hung and underwear for a few days can fit into a bedside table with a decent drawer.

☐ Beds on legs are good, as suitcases can be pushed underneath and stowed away.

☐ Years ago, I read about a 'Granny Box'. This was a box with shampoo, slippers, a decent mirror and perhaps a nightie and dressing gown. It means granny – or any other guest – won't have to bring extra luggage when they come to stay and can just focus on carrying the clothes they want to wear.

☐ A pretty bowl filled with samples of shampoo, cleansers and moisturizers from magazines and makeup buying trips will make the guest room feel a bit 'hotel', while a selection of paperback books on a shelf is always welcome.

☐ If you can fit a wall-mounted television this can be great for grandparents who are coming to stay – and who might find small children a little too much by the feral hour of 6pm. They can take a gin upstairs and watch the news while you make dinner. Or, in your dreams, the other way around.

ON HOW TO MIX AND CLASH
DIFFERENT COLOURS
AND PRINTS

Just as the no-makeup makeup look requires as much, if not more, product as a full face for a night out, so the mixing of patterns and colours involves more work than its seemingly casual composition might imply.

- Identify your starting point – this might be a cushion, rug or painting. Look at the colours within it to create your basic palette. This will probably give you around three to seven different shades. I tend to pick three, used in varying tones, with a couple more as accents.

- Once you've decided on the basic palette, you can start to bring in different prints and textures. Try the 60-30-10 rule. This will roughly translate as the most amount of colour (60%) on the largest space (usually the walls), with the next layer (30%) on the second largest space (the floor), and finally a touch (10%) of the colour you want to use least. For example, yellow might be too much for all four walls, so keep it to the accessories.

- When it comes to mixing patterns, you can put large florals with geometrics and stripes. It's harder to mix tiny floral prints as they tend to wash out from a distance and the whole thing can look bitty and messy, rather than bold and exuberant. If you have fallen in love with a small print, use it in decent quantities so it doesn't disappear, then add extras to highlight it in the same way that a bright blue scarf would highlight the blue eyes of the wearer. For instance, you could cover an armchair in a small print you love and then use bold blocks of colour on its cushions or fringing to emphasize it.

- Try mixing stripes of different widths as well as colours, but make sure that you never lose sight of the basic palette. Think of it as a chain: take one pattern with, say, five colours, and link three of those colours to something in a geometric pattern, then take two of those colours in plain weaves and sit them next to a stripe of one of the colours and a neutral. That way you can trace a link from the busiest design to the most pared back.

- Finally, remember to mix up the textiles. For example, a linen floral and a cotton stripe with a plain velvet. The best way to ensure it works is to put all the fabric samples together against a piece of card painted in the colour of the walls. Cut the swatches to proportional sizes – a large piece for a sofa, a smaller one for a cushion – so that you can see it all together before you commit to spending any money.

THE SIX QUESTIONS

WHO?

WHAT?

WHEN?

You must ask and, crucially, answer these six questions honestly before you start any decorating if a room is to reflect the style and suit the needs of those who use it.

WHERE?

WHY?

HOW?

LUST, LOVE, LOATHE...

LUST

_____
_____
_____
_____
_____
_____
_____

LOVE

_____
_____
_____
_____
_____
_____
_____

LOATHE

_____
_____
_____
_____
_____
_____
_____

The interior design version of 'Kiss, Marry, Kill'. Make a note of your aspirations for the space, the great features of the room and the things you want to replace.

Use fabric swatches to make cushions – they don't have to match front and back and you effectively get two for one.

9 THE HOME OFFICE

The home office has often been relegated to the smallest space in the house. I've seen them in nooks under the eaves and under stairs, in rooms with tiny windows, and in (literal) spare rooms. In the latter, the desk often shares space with the unused double guest bed, the laundry rack, and that pile of stuff waiting to go to the charity shop. It was often only those who worked from home full time that had anything approaching a proper office and, according to a 2019 UK study, that was only 5.1 per cent of the population. Then Covid-19 struck and suddenly the whole world worked from home. And the world's children were schooled at home. And the world of home offices had to change.

So, this is a room that has taken on greater significance than we might ever have imagined. The key thing to consider is what you need to help you work. For me it's about always wearing shoes (not slippers), putting on some makeup and some proper clothes. It's about taking proper breaks from my desk and using the 'commute' to do some morning exercises or, later on, to change into more relaxed evening clothes or have a cocktail. Perching on the sofa with the laptop balanced on the coffee table might work for a week, but it's not comfortable for a career. It doesn't matter if it's a whole room or a desk in a cupboard that you can shut away at the end of the day, if you want to get the most out of your home office you need to take some time to plan it. Imagine if your boss said you had unlimited budget and space in return for working a 15-hour day. What would you ask for? And can you bring some of that to your office space?

One of the key things to remember is that your work space needs to be inspirational. It doesn't matter how small it is, you need to feel happy and ready to work when you sit down – and not dread going in there so much you end up hotdesking from the sofa or kitchen table.

A survey quoted in *My Creative Space: How to Design Your Home to Stimulate Ideas and Spark Innovation* by Donald M. Rattner found the traditional office ranks towards the bottom of the list of places where people gain creative insights. Instead, according to the data, it's far more likely you'll be at home or doing something associated with residential life during moments of illumination. So, by that token, getting the home office right is an all-round winner.

Yes, it has to be functional, but it must also be inspirational. Studies have found that we work better if we think of something nostalgic before starting a creative task. Have pictures of happy memories around you. If you don't have a window, then a picture with a view of an outside space can help.

INSPIRING OFFICE SPACES: A CHECKLIST

It may be an office but it's still your home, so make sure the room or area fits in with the rest of the house. Pieces that reflect your style and taste will inspire you, and create a space that pleases you, which will result in better, more efficient work.

☐ Choose your space wisely. It needs to feel like a workstation, so whether you have the luxury of a whole 'spare' room or a table in a corner, make sure you will be comfortable there for several hours.

☐ If the office space is in your bedroom or living room, you need to find a way to screen it off at the end of the day. Building an office into a cupboard or alcove, even a wardrobe, is a good way to do this.

☐ You don't have to work in the same place you store your work stuff. Sometimes the kitchen table is just the best and lightest place to work, but keeping the paperwork elsewhere will at least add to the number of daily steps you take. As will putting it away afterwards.

☐ The cupboard under the stairs may be great for office storage, but you probably won't want to sit in there all day. So, kit it out as a walk-in filing cabinet and carry your laptop elsewhere. Alternatively, remove the doors, install some shelving and turn the under-stairs space into a beautiful designated workstation.

☐ Take time to consider what colours make you feel happy, inspired or energized.

☐ Buy the biggest desk you can fit into the space and consider having a functional office chair reupholstered in a fabulous print that you will enjoy looking at.

☐ Lighting is key. If your desk is too small for a task light, consider hanging one from the ceiling to drop down low over the desk.

☐ A desk with drawers is a quick way to clear up at the end of the day – especially if the office needs to revert to a dining room or living room at 5pm.

☐ Don't forget the walls – if you run out of horizontal storage then shelves, corkboards and chalk boards can all be pressed into service.

ON HOW TO CREATE
A PROFESSIONAL WORKING SPACE

In recent times, working from home (WFH) has become much more accepted. Employers have realized that not everyone needs to be in the office all the time and we have all become much more adept at dialling into meetings via our computers. But if you are one of the WFH brigade, you need to get your office space sorted out. While it can be amusing to get a glimpse of people's décor, pets and small children, if you're hoping to make working from home a regular fixture, make sure it looks professional.

- By now we have all got used to the idea of curating our backgrounds but do be aware of it. You won't go wrong with a plain white wall (unless you are an interior designer), but equally you want to move that wonky lampshade and pile of drying laundry. Books, if you check first, are usually a fairly safe option and give an air of intelligence. Wallpaper brings a decorative touch and may give people something to talk about.

- If you are working in your bedroom, take time to ensure that anything 'bedroomy' is out of shot, or make sure you move the laptop around to cut the unused exercise bike out of the picture.

- Use leftover paint to add a rectangle of colour on the wall and hang pictures within it.

- Plants clean the air, reduce stress and look good. Bring them into your office and include them in your virtual background. Even the person looking at your plants via your screen will feel better, so they might help you clinch that deal.

- Sit as close to a natural light source as possible and if the sun is shining directly in, try hanging a sheet in front of it to soften it. If it's dark, then point your desk lamp at the wall in front of you so the reflected light will bounce softly back onto your face.

- Make sure your chair is the right height: your feet should be flat on the floor, your knees and elbows at right angles, with the latter level with the keyboard (use hand rests if necessary). The computer monitor should be an arm's length away and slightly lower than your eyes when you are sitting upright (which you should be).

- And finally, although this is less décor than general advice, remember to prop your laptop up on a sturdy pile of books. I have seen up more peoples' noses during Zoom meetings than is necessary or advisable. Your posture will also thank you.

THE SIX QUESTIONS

WHO?

WHAT?

WHEN?

You must ask and, crucially, answer these six questions honestly before you start any decorating if a room is to reflect the style and suit the needs of those who use it.

WHERE?

WHY?

HOW?

LUST, LOVE, LOATHE...

LUST

_____
_____
_____
_____
_____

LOVE

_____
_____
_____
_____
_____

LOATHE

_____
_____
_____
_____
_____

The interior design version of 'Kiss, Marry, Kill'. Make a note of your aspirations for the space, the great features of the room and the things you want to replace.

Keep track of your stationery by buying a set of those clear Perspex drawers from Muji – that way you can see where everything is at a glance and don't have to rummage through drawers and piles of paper.

10 YOUR HOME, YOUR LISTS

I'm hoping that by the time you reach this chapter, you'll have planned your room(s), pulled your design together and worked out everything you love, loathe and lust after. Here is where you'll find checklists, tips and advice for the final planning stages and perfect finishing touches. I've also given you space to record those all-important paint colours (the ones that took countless test pots to find), a place to plan your budget and keep a running total of what you've spent so far, as well as your very own 'little black book' to safely store the details of all the trades, stores and suppliers you love. It's everything you need for your home to tell your story.

As I said at the beginning, the graph paper is intended as a place for you to create your floor plans, but it also works as a spreadsheet. So I've set aside a page or two to keep a record of what you have spent or quotes you have received against what it actually cost. That will help you keep track of the budget and work out if there's anything left over for shoes.

There is space to write down the contact details of your favourite tradesmen, but how do you find a good one? Word of mouth is always best but check also if they have an Instagram account. Are they proud of their work and wanting to show it off? That is always a good sign.

If you're feeling overwhelmed (and with big projects we all hit a wall at some point), use the Lust, Love, Loathe pages in each chapter to go back and read over what you wanted for the space – and to remind yourself how far you've come. If you're stuck for inspiration I always find it helps to write a list. Make a cup of coffee, scroll through Instagram or Pinterest and use one of the blank pages to write down how certain colours and styles make you feel. When you read back over your notes, you will have created a much clearer idea of the direction you want to go in, and how to get there.

A virtual moodboard is a good starting point, but you need to see the colours and touch the fabrics in real life. Once you have sorted out the basics, request the samples and put them together. This will help you see if there is too much of one colour, or if another needs boosting, or if you need more variety of texture. Keep a note of the final choices so you can always refer back to it.

☐ Go Large. Buy the biggest rug you can afford, the largest mirror, the enormous paper lantern – even one that looks slightly too big for the space. Large will attract attention (thus diverting it from the old sofa, or wonky coffee table). It will feel luxurious and provide the focal point. Even a huge vase filled with dried flowers will look dramatic and confident. Far better a single large object than a collection of fussy things that will always make visitors worry about breakages.

☐ Big rugs are expensive but, again, they talk of luxury and wealth – not just financially but also in a tactile sense. If you can't find, or afford, a rug that is big enough for the space, buy a large piece of carpet and have the edges hemmed (your local carpet shop should be able to help with this). Now that lots of companies are making patterned carpet, you should be able to find something that looks less carpet and more rug. The bespoke nature of the hem – in a contrasting colour or wide band – will also look luxurious.

☐ Mirrors are brilliant for reflecting light around a room and bouncing it back from windows and open doors. They can be expensive but there are workarounds. Buy a large picture from a junk shop and replace the image with a mirror. Stick foxed, or aged, mirror tiles to the wall and frame them with cheap architrave. The designer Orla Kiely bought an elaborate vintage door frame, stuck a piece of wood along the bottom to complete it, and filled it with mirror. It's a stunning piece of furniture that she then propped in front of an ugly fireplace to hide it.

☐ Get the lighting right. Good lighting will make everything in the room look better, particularly at night when a soft ambient glow will flatter a multitude of budget furniture sins. Make sure you have lamps at different heights, throwing out light at different angles – washing down over a picture or up over the curtains. And don't forget to leave the odd dark corner. It will look mysterious and enticing. And confident.

☐ Change the handles. Just as your canny grandmother might have suggested you change the buttons on a cheap cardigan to make it look more expensive, so changing the handles can make a world of difference to an unattractive door or kitchen cupboard. The handles on my first Ikea kitchen were all black leather straps, which added a tactile element to the space. Leather also improves with age and abuse so it's not as impractical as it may sound.

- [ ] Make sure the paintwork is clean and tidy. Nothing looks worse than neglected and scuffed paintwork. Touch up and redo as often as you can face it.

- [ ] Houseplants are having a moment – and not just because they are proven to clean the air and remove toxins. A room filled with healthy thriving plants will always look more enticing. But I mean healthy and thriving. They need water and large leaves need dusting. Plants also subscribe to the first point on 'going large', too. A tray of small succulents looks student, a massive fiddle-leaf fig looks expensive and luxurious.

- [ ] Sort your artwork out. At the risk of sounding controversial, I'm not a fan of buying lots of cheap prints and framing them. To start with, you run the risk that everyone else has the same thing. But nor am I suggesting you need to spend a fortune on 'art'. Frame a poster from the museum shop, the ticket from the first gig you went to with your partner, a drawing by one of your kids... but put them in a good mount to make them look more expensive. Museum shops are great places to hunt for postcards by famous artists – you might not be able to afford a painting, but a set of postcards can be just as effective framed. Think also about mounting vintage magazine covers and framing tea towels. All this will create a collection that is personal to you and that will always look better.

- [ ] Something vintage will always elevate a space. It's great if it belonged to your granny, but it's fine if it belonged to someone else's and came from eBay. A find like this will bring character and is more likely to be a one-off. The key is that your house doesn't look like the one next door, even if they are the same shape.

- [ ] Nothing says expensive, airy and luxurious more than fresh air and clean windows letting the light stream in. You wouldn't go out in a fabulous dress for an evening out without washing your hair, would you? Because in the end, it all comes down to the details. No one will notice your cheap sofa if the room is light and airy, smells fresh, is well maintained and tells a story, either through the interesting works of art, the one-off pieces of furniture, or the sense of welcoming luxury underfoot.

on CLEARING UP
and CLEARING OUT

When the boys were small, I used to do a frantic clear out before Christmas to make room for the deluge of new stuff that was about to arrive. Out went the toys that were no longer played with, the clothes that were too small, and the kitchen gadgets that take up precious cupboard space and are never used – juicer anyone? To help when you're having a clear out, here are some ideas to give your items a new lease of life...

- The first port of call is often the charity shop and they don't always want your stuff. There are rules about what they can accept – a valid fire label, for instance, is vital – and they can often be overwhelmed with items that people can't be bothered to sort themselves. If you are getting rid of jigsaws with missing pieces, stained cushions and a lamp that no longer works, sort it all out into different materials and take it to the local waste and recycling centre, where they can recycle and reduce the amount going to landfill.
- To donate furniture, you can first ask your local council if they can use it. Then you can see if there is an Emmaus local to you. This French organization was founded after WWII in Paris by the French Resistance fighter Abbé Pierre to provide homes for homeless people. Now Emmaus International brings together 410 associations in 41 countries, spread over 4 continents. It came to the UK in the 1990s and there are now 29 communities spread across the UK, supporting some 750 people by giving them a home for as long as they need it and work in the Emmaus community. They also save some 3,000 tonnes of furniture from landfill annually.
- You can also book a collection from the Furniture Donation Network. They will collect items of furniture from inside your home (so you don't need to heave it about). They then either donate it to low-income families or sell it to help with social welfare projects.
- Another idea is the Reuse Network, which helps families in crisis by putting them in contact with places where they can find affordable (sometimes free) items for their homes and, vice versa, help families find a local place to donate things they no longer need.
- There is also the Veterans Charity, who provide furniture and other essentials – food, clothing and household goods – as well as Forces Support, who will collect furniture and carry out house clearances.
- The British Heart Foundation will also collect unwanted items such as mirrors, vases and ornaments.
- When it comes to paint, liquids are banned from landfill so the council cannot accept paint until it has hardened. You can try adding soil or sand to the tin to speed this process up. If you have a decent amount of paint left over, contact Community RePaint – a UK-wide network of over 75 schemes who collect surplus and leftover paint and then make it available to individuals and families in social need. They also supply community groups and charities, so the surplus paint can be redirected to projects such as decorating community centres and creating colourful playground murals.

If you are starting the room from scratch, begin with the floor plan (see page 9). You need to plan where the furniture is going before you can light it.

☐ Remember that a floor plan is a 2D aerial view, whereas you will be in the room looking at the walls. So, don't plan for a symmetrical grid of downlights, but think about where in the room they will be needed. The chances are the answer is not a symmetrical grid.

☐ If you are putting downlights in rooms other than kitchens and bathrooms, try and keep them to the edges – about 30cm (12in) in from the edge of the ceiling. This works for a bedroom too, as you don't want to be dazzled when you are lying down.

☐ Place a downlight over the centre of a window, which will wash light down over your curtains. This saves you from worrying about exactly where you might hang a picture, and then from the feeling you can't move it because of the light.

☐ Downlights should be on a dimmer so you can change the atmosphere easily.

☐ If you are lighting a large room – or a multi-purpose one like a kitchen diner – then put lights on different circuits so you can dim the area over the washing up while you are having dinner, for example. Alternatively, just have a couple of dim lights by the sofa when you are watching TV.

☐ Most rooms won't allow for lots of different furniture configurations, so consider a downlight over a coffee table to highlight anything you are displaying there, or to throw light over the Lego model or the half-finished jigsaw puzzle – ambient light is never enough to find that last piece.

☐ Only once you have planned the fixed lights can you start to think about placing table lamps and floor lamps for atmosphere.

☐ Don't be afraid to leave a dark corner. This hints at mystery and also implies that the room might actually be larger than it is, as you aren't highlighting every nook and cranny.

MAD ABOUT THE HOUSE: THE DIRECTORY

ART

Jealous Gallery
jealousgallery.com

Oneoffto25
(for limited edition art)
oneoffto25.com

Print Sisters Archive
printsistersarchive.com

Rise Art
riseart.com

BEDDING

Rise & Fall
(for organic cotton sheets)
riseandfall.co

Society of Wanderers
societyofwanderers.com

HOMEWARE

La Redoute
laredoute.co.uk

Muji
mujionline.eu/uk

Polkra
polkra.com

Rockett St George
rockettstgeorge.co.uk

Rose & Grey
roseandgrey.co.uk

Rowen & Wren
rowenandwren.co.uk

WA Green
wagreen.co.uk

West Elm
westelm.co.uk

Zara Home
zarahome.com/gb

LIGHTING

Bespoke Binny
bespokebinny.com

houseof
houseof.com

MatchiMatchi
matchimatchi.com

Original BTC
(for UK-made heritage
lighting) originalbtc.com

Pooky
pooky.com

TILES

Ca' Pietra
capietra.com

Claybrook
claybrookstudio.co.uk

Topps Tiles
toppstiles.co.uk

WALLPAPER AND FABRIC

Divine Savages
divinesavages.com

Haines Collections
(for surplus fabric left
over from interior design
schemes and remnants)
hainescollection.co.uk

Ottoline
ottoline.co.uk

VINTAGE

Home Barn
homebarnshop.co.uk

Lovely & Co
lovelyandco.co.uk

MoseyHome
moseyhome.co.uk

The Peanut Vendor
thepeanutvendor.co.uk

Vinterior
vinterior.co

SOFAS AND CHAIRS

Love Your Home
love-your-home.co.uk

Ochre
ochre.net

Pinch
pinchdesign.com

DESIGN STOREY

designstorey.shop

This is my tightly curated edit of everything for the home. You'll find the 50 best of each home product – from lamps and cushions to tables and chairs. It's a department store for the 21st century.

KEY MEASUREMENTS

_____
_____
_____
_____
_____
_____
_____
_____
_____
_____
_____
_____
_____

SMART SHIPPING

If you're looking for vintage and second-hand items, many pieces online are 'collection only', but these days that needn't be a deal-breaker. In the UK, companies like Shiply and AnyVan will bid to transport your table from Billericay to Brighton, and only set off when they've filled their trucks. You explain what needs moving, where from, where to, and when by, and they come back to you with quotes on what it will cost. The model relies on them filling a van with things and dropping off and picking up in a round trip. So, it's economically priced and environmentally friendlier, as you're waiting for a whole van to be filled rather than paying for a single journey with one table on board.

   Usually the more flexible you can be and the longer you can wait, the better the price. I paid £50 to get my six mid-century dining chairs from Sheffield to London in three days. I could have paid less but I decided to go with the mid-price and the best reviews – interestingly neither the company offering the most expensive nor the cheapest quote had better reviews. Once again, a quick burst of research will pay dividends. Do they have the best reviews? Do they wrap the furniture in blankets? Will they bring it into the house or leave it on the pavement. Check the details and choose the courier that meets your needs.

ADDRESS BOOK (STORES)

ADDRESS BOOK (WEBSITES)

ADDRESS BOOK (TRADES)

_____
_____
_____
_____
_____
_____
_____
_____
_____
_____
_____
_____
_____
_____
_____
_____
_____
_____

Look for a builder with an Instagram account or one who will take the time to show you pictures of their previous projects – this shows they take pride in their work and that counts for a lot.

ADDRESS BOOK (ENERGY SUPPLIERS)

_____

_____

_____

_____

A list for you to make as the information changes all the time

_____

_____

_____

_____

_____

_____

_____

_____

_____

_____

_____

_____

_____

_____

BEST GREEN ENERGY SUPPLIERS

Many of us are becoming more aware of where our energy is coming from, and there are so many benefits to switching to a green supplier – from contributing to a cleaner planet to cheaper energy bills. Suppliers change all the time, so do your research and check an independent consumer advice website, like Which?, to find the most up-to-date information available.

PAINT DIRECTORY

Name	Brand	Cost	Room / Amount

PAINT: A PRACTICAL GUIDE

WHICH PAINT IS BEST FOR WHICH SURFACE?

As a rough guide, you usually want emulsion for walls. The fashionable chalky, matt-finish paint is not very hardwearing, so keep it to bedrooms and living rooms. For halls and kitchens, you need a slight sheen, as this is tougher and wipes clean. Eggshell is for wood and metal, so you will need to buy this for radiators and doors. Emulsion will chip off very easily. Gloss is the toughest and takes ages to dry. It's also hardest to apply to get a good finish. It has fallen out of fashion for woodwork these days, but that is its traditional use. However, I have seen gloss used in hallways to bounce light around dark spaces and provide a tough finish against scuffs. I have also used eggshell on Anaglypta wallpaper to give an extra sheen, and an increasing number of design types also use eggshell on ceilings to bounce the light around. To go one step further, a gloss ceiling will look wonderful if your surface is super flat and will give the appearance of lacquer. It will show every lump and bump if it's not smooth though, so avoid gloss if you're working with old plaster or textured wallpaper.

ECO PAINT COMPANIES

Many companies are trying to reduce their impact on the planet. Here is a list of eco paint companies to try:

COAT (coatpaints.com)
Edward Bulmer (edwardbulmerpaint.co.uk)
Farrow & Ball (farrow-ball.com)
Frenchic Furniture Paint (frenchicpaint.co.uk)
Graphenstone (graphenstone.co.uk)
Lakeland Paints (lakelandpaints.co.uk)
Lick (lickhome.com)
Little Greene (littlegreene.com)
Mylands (mylands.com)
Paint & Paper Library (paintandpaperlibrary.com)
Painthouse (painthouse.co.uk)
Paint the Town Green (paintthetowngreen.co.uk)

DO LESS HARM DIRECTORY (madaboutthehouse.com/do-less-harm/)
This is my directory of companies that are genuinely trying to Do Less Harm. It covers everything from paint and flooring to fabric and furniture. I wanted you to be able to find out what companies are doing to reduce their impact on the planet. So when you shop you will know what questions to ask and can base your purchasing decisions, not just on the colour and size of the new item you want, but also perhaps on the type of packaging it will arrive in and what will happen to the old one if they take it away.

BUDGET

BUDGET

A NOTE ON DIMENSIONS AND REGULATIONS

The ideas and advice in this book have no regard for geographic boundaries. Smart design is smart design. Dimensions and construction specifics may differ however. So you need to do your homework.

Wherever you live, keep in mind that not all building codes are the same in every area. Codes and restrictions might even vary from town to town or state to state. Some areas may have extra restrictions depending on designated flood zones and historical preservation districts. Other neighbourhoods may have covenants limiting building heights, materials used and even choice of paint colour. You should also be mindful of the environmental impact of your design choices.

While you don't need to apply for a permit to change a light bulb or a light fixture, performing your own electrical work on more complex tasks brings with it a number of safety risks. Even if your local building codes do not require electrical work be done by a licensed professional, it's likely that any work done by an unlicensed worker will still have to be checked by the building inspector. Avoid the hassle and hire a professional at the outset.

Similarly, before you make a wood-burning stove the focal point of your living area, do your research and ensure the stove will meet the national environmental standards and comply with all of the relevant installation and safety regulations.

Whatever the size and scope of your project, it's always best to seek out professional input. YouTube videos cannot solve every problem. Work with experienced contractors and tradespeople from your area who are familiar with local building codes and regulations. It helps if your team has a good working relationship with the building inspector as well.

MATTRESS SIZES

A king-size mattress in Canada is at least a foot wider than the British king-size version. When you're planning a bedroom, remember to factor in how much space the mattress plus bed frame will need.

Standard Mattress Sizes UK
Single 91 x 190cm (36 x 75in)
Double 137 x 190cm (54 x 75in)
King 152 x 198cm (60 x 78in)

Standard Mattress Sizes US and Canada
Twin 38 x 75in
Full (aka double) 53 x 75in
Queen 60 x 80in
King 75 x 80in

KITCHEN CABINET SIZES

You'll find a wide range of configurations when buying pre-fab cabinetry.

UK

A kitchen cupboard is usually 60cm (23½in) wide and deep, but Ikea makes 40cm (16in) and 20cm (8in) variants. You can, of course, go bespoke, but knowing this will give you a rough idea of how much storage you can fit in at a glance.

US and Canada

Base cabinets: The standard height of the base cabinet is 34.5in without the countertop, 36in with the countertop. The toekick at the bottom measures 4.5in. Standard depth is 24in. Widths range from 9in to 47in: the most popular are 30in and 36in wide.

Upper cabinets: Standard heights are 30in, 36in or 42in. Standard depth is 12in. Some go up to 24in deep to accommodate installation over a refrigerator or wall-mounted oven. Many manufacturers offer custom sizes as well without too great an upcharge.

BATH SIZES

UK

A bath is usually 1700 x 700mm (67 x 27½in), and a short one tends to be 1500mm (59in) long but the same width (700mm/27½in). A large one is 1800 x 800mm (71 x 31½in).

US

A standard wall-to-wall bathtub measures 60in long and 30in to 32in wide. But today's bathtubs come in a number of nonstandard shapes and sizes from cozy corner tubs to small alcove tubs to oversized, free-standing oval tubs.

MORE MAD ABOUT THE HOUSE

Find even more ideas and interiors inspiration in my previous books...
Mad About the House: How to Decorate Your Home with Style
Mad About the House: 101 Interior Design Answers

Follow me on Instagram @mad_about_the_house
Keep up with the blog at madaboutthehouse.com
Listen to the The Great Indoors podcast – a celebration of all things interiors. In each episode, I discuss, debate and guide you through the top trends and hottest topics from the home front alongside co-host Sophie Robinson.

DESIGN FOR DIVERSITY
I launched Design For Diversity with interior designer Rukmini Patel in June 2020 following the global Black Lives Matter protests after the murder of George Floyd in Minneapolis, when a police officer knelt on his neck for more than eight minutes after he told them: 'I can't breathe.'

Sophie Robinson and I dedicated an episode of The Great Indoors podcast to voices from the Black, Asian and Ethnic Minority community about their experiences in the field of interiors. It was both shocking and heart-breaking to hear their stories. So Rukmini and I set up the pledge, a three-point promise covering visibility, opportunity and accessibility within the sector, and a sign, symbolized by a sticker, that brands, businesses and bloggers can display to show they are are committed to working towards a diverse design industry. It had over 150 sign-ups in the first month and has led to companies setting up mentoring programmes, arranging student bursaries and employing designers from a more diverse range of backgrounds. Read about the pledge at madaboutthehouse.com or rukminipatel.com

ACKNOWLEDGEMENTS

Writing a book is about so much more than the words. It involves a whole team, and putting a book together during a global pandemic requires even more effort. The idea for this book had been bubbling for a while and it felt like the perfect next step in the *Mad About The House* series. First, find your style, second answer all those questions, and finally a place to keep all those notes and ideas for your own space. But then the world shut down. The contract was signed in the first week of lockdown and I wrote furiously (both literally and metaphorically) while attending Zoom meetings, holding colour swatches and ribbons up to the screen and debating the perfect size for a graph paper square without being able to just draw it and push it across a table.

But we did it. And Abi Read did her usual brilliant illustrations (this time blank in case you want to colour them in). And Krissy Mallett edited and improved my words so patiently and beautifully, while Laura Russell understood my vision so perfectly and pulled all the design elements together exactly how I imagined. Thanks also to my editor, Lucy Smith, and Helen Lewis, my publisher, who got behind the idea of a book of blank pages, to Jane Turnbull, my agent, for being such an enthusiastic reader and supporter of my ideas, and Frida Green for organizing publicity for the last book when no parties or events were allowed.

To my friends, whom I have barely seen in real life for so long, and my readers, without whom none of this would be possible, thank you all for being there.

And finally, to my husband, Ad, and my sons Isaac and Noah. You are everything.